ROLLING STONES

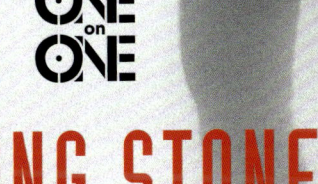

ROLLING STONES

GERED MANKOWITZ

Essay by Sean Egan

INSIGHT ◉ EDITIONS

San Rafael, California

INSIGHT  **EDITIONS**

PO Box 3088 • San Rafael • CA 94912
www.insighteditions.com

Library of Congress Cataloging-in-Publication
Data available.

ISBN: 978-1-60887-091-2

ROOTS of PEACE   🌲 REPLANTED PAPER

Insight Editions, in association with Roots of Peace,
will plant two trees for each tree used in the manufac-
turing of this book. Roots of Peace is an internation-
ally renowned humanitarian organization dedicated
to eradicating land mines worldwide and converting
war-torn lands into productive farms and wildlife habi-
tats. Together, we will plant two million fruit and nut
trees in Afghanistan and provide farmers there with the
skills and support necessary for sustainable land use.

Manufactured in China by Insight Editions

10 9 8 7 6 5 4 3 2 1

CONTENTS

PREFACE

Without Chad and Jeremy, this book might not have existed. Chad and Jeremy were much more successful in the U.S. than they were here at home in the UK, but for the first year or so of their career, as a sweet-sounding folk/pop duo, I was their photographer and became a close friend.

Jeremy was very much the 1960's epitome of a "ladies man," tall and slim, charming and funny, with an aristocratic air that came from a public school education and the fact that he was the grandson of the then Duke of Wellington. During a spring 1964 appearance on the very popular TV show *Thank Your Lucky Stars* to promote their single "Yesterday's Gone," Jeremy met Marianne Faithfull, who was performing her first

single "As Tears Go By." For some reason Marianne was by herself and rather nervous, and Jeremy took her under his protective wing.

We had arranged to meet at Jeremy's apartment that same evening. I was hanging out with his flat-mate when Jeremy and Marianne arrived off the Birmingham train after the show broadcast.

I was captivated by Marianne from the moment I first saw her. She was beautiful, funny, and bright, and I immediately persuaded her to let me photograph her the following day. I took her to a location I liked, and we had a great first session together. She was a joy to photograph, and there seemed to be some real connection between us.

A few days later she invited me to attend a recording session at Decca Studios. After I photographed her there, we did a couple of sessions in my Mason's Yard studio, and then I decided to shoot some portraits in a wonderful pub called the Salisbury on St. Martin's Lane in London's West End. She was working on her first album, and I hoped that we might possibly get an image that would work for a cover.

Marianne had been discovered by Andrew Loog Oldham and was managed through his office. Andrew didn't involve himself with the day-to-day management, so I hadn't run into him yet, although his reputation was well known to me. Apparently Andrew loved the Salisbury pub portraits of Marianne, and he asked me to come to his office in Gloucester Place so we could talk about the possibility of working with his other band — the Rolling Stones.

I had met Rolling Stone Brian Jones earlier in the year at a restaurant and had found him charming and amusing. I was actually a fan of the band — possibly the only time that I would ever have described myself as such — from the first moment I saw them on TV, so the possibility of working with them at this early stage of my career was very exciting.

The first meeting in Andrew's office was nerve-wracking. The band was very nice to me, and we all seemed to get on rather well, so I quickly felt at ease. This was at the end of 1964, and I was just eighteen years old! We agreed to shoot my first session with them early in the following year at my studio in Mason's Yard, after they had returned from their Australian tour and around the time that their single "The Last Time" was released in the UK.

For the better part of the following three years I remained their photographer, shooting with them on tour, backstage, in the recording studio, in my studio, on location, and at home.

It was all an incredibly exciting, extraordinary experience, and I hope my photos allow readers to share some of that excitement.

—Gered Mankowitz

1965

IN EARLY 1965, NORTH LONDONER Gered Mankowitz was eighteen years old. In 1962, he had emerged from a photography apprenticeship provided by his mentor Tom Blau of the agency Camera Press, and since then he had started to have a little success, snapping folk duo Chad and Jeremy, working for their label Ember records, and shooting beautiful chanteuse Marianne Faithfull. Says Mankowitz, "I'd already made a transition from what I thought was going to be a career as a theatrical photographer into music, which was the most exciting area of showbiz for somebody of my age. It was where everything fell into place." However, via his work for another client of Faithfull's manager Andrew Loog Oldham, he was about to be catapulted into the stratosphere.

Says Mankowitz, "Andrew thought that I had a rawness, a quality to my photography that would somehow work with the Stones." The Rolling Stones were something out of the ordinary in popular music terms. The Beatles' mop-top haircuts were cute, but the collar-brushing locks of the Stones were brutal-looking for the times, while their individualistic dress took some getting used to in a pop scene where no previous ensemble had done anything other than sport a group uniform. Once society had negotiated the Stones' visual appearance, it had to deal with their attitudes: They were outspoken about individual rights at a point in history when conformity was considered less a virtue than proof of a lack of complete degeneracy.

Mankowitz's studio was located in Mason's Yard, then littered with building-site paraphernalia. He decided to utilize this backdrop for his first Rolling Stones session because he thought it provided the appropriate ambience for a band considered so uncouth and rebellious that the previous week the press had branded them animals for their behavior when refused permission to a garage lavatory. One of the resultant pictures found the Stones peering at the viewer through what seemed a three-sided tunnel. Mankowitz explains that the effect was achieved by "the hoardings that were removed during the day that actually protected the building site at night. They were just stacked randomly against a wall, and I saw this deep triangular shape and got the guys to pose for me at the other end of it. I knew that that was going to work for a record cover, if I was lucky enough to get it, because it gave natural places to put the band's name and the logo and all that stuff. That was crucial in those days because record covers weren't conceived or planned." Oldham did indeed consider one of the shots cover-worthy and used it on the September 1965 UK LP *Out of Our Heads* and the U.S. album *December's Children*. Mankowitz says, "That was a huge, huge breakthrough for me and confirmation that I was doing something right."

Mankowitz was now part of the Stones' circle and their in-house man-with-a-camera. He found himself shooting a group of men who were each in his own way visually compelling. Of blond guitarist Brian Jones, Mankowitz notes, "He was the most photogenic, and I felt that he was the most defined at that first session I did. Brian had a definite pop star element to him with his hair and his white trousers and his funny shoes. Having said that, when you look at the pictures, Charlie [Watts, drummer] is very formed, very rounded in terms of his personal image because he was the jazz freak and had adopted this hip, New York look. Bill [Wyman, bassist] was always rather eccentric and had his own unique look. Keith and Mick still looked a bit student-like."

Lead singer Mick Jagger was a celebrity like none before, in that many experienced difficulty deciding whether he was handsome or ugly. Mankowitz: "He had one of those faces that was teetering on the brink of ugliness: the mouth was too full and his on-stage performance had

"The Rolling Stones were something out of the ordinary in popular music terms."

elements of grotesqueness to it. I think, actually, in repose he was very beautiful." Meanwhile, though guitarist Keith Richards would develop by the seventies an iconic, swaggering rock 'n' roll outlaw image, Mankowitz says, "He was gauche in the beginning because there was an innocence and a naïveté to everybody: nobody really knew where this was going." He adds, though, "Interestingly, [Keith] transformed very quickly. By the end of '65, he was looking pretty cool and stylish. What was happening was happening quite quickly. "

When Mankowitz hooked up with the Stones, they were still essentially a covers band. That changed over the course of 1965 as the Jagger-Richards songwriting axis not only developed but began turning out records like "(I Can't Get No) Satisfaction" and "Get Off of My Cloud," both cast-iron classics and belligerent anthems that summed up the frustrations of an emerging generation unwilling to accept the strictures endured by their parents. So dramatic was their blossoming that the Stones finished the year in cultural importance behind only the Beatles and Bob Dylan. This was reflected in their reception on their American tour of October–December 1965, the band's fourth but Mankowitz's first negotiation of that country. "I think Andrew wanted me on because the Beatles had had their photographer Dezo Hoffman earlier in the year," he says. The Stones "were enormously successful in America because 'Satisfaction' had already been a hit, and 'Get Off of My Cloud' was going to be number one during the tour."

In retrospect, Mankowitz finds it extraordinary that with Oldham already in New York setting things up with Stones comanager Allen Klein, the touring party consisted merely of the band, roadie Ian Stewart, and him-self. With his access-all-areas status ("I was treated as another member of the band"), Mankowitz was able to capture some candid shots. However, being a friend of the group engendered what some might consider an unavoidable dishonesty: scenes with groupies and drugs were part of the tour's reality but not recorded by him. "I didn't see it as being dishonest in any way,"

"The stones were one of the biggest propositions going, and this was their first tour with their own private plane."

Mankowitz shrugs. "I'm not instinctively a paparazzi-type photographer. The hotel rooms were private. I was so inept as a photojournalist that I didn't walk around with a camera around my neck all the time. So when we were in New York and Brian Jones said, 'Do you want to meet Bob Dylan?' I didn't have a camera with me. Yet that moment was rock 'n' roll history."

The Stones were one of the biggest propositions going, and this was their first tour with their own private plane, but rock music was still deemed the poor relation of the entertainment industry, and this was reflected in the sometimes ramshackle nature of the sojourn. Explains Mankowitz, "The promoters in America, a lot of them were amateurs who were more used to putting on a rodeo or a wrestling match." He remembers the venues were "quite a mixture. I don't think anything was much bigger than two- or three-thousand seaters. They were playing theaters and small sports arenas. Mick sang through the house PA. They didn't carry their own sound system. They didn't carry their own lights. They would perform in front of whatever backing the venue put up, sometimes just a black curtain, sometimes a red curtain. I don't remember a sound check in the auditorium ever. They would tune up in the dressing room.

"The lighting was so awful — perhaps just one follow spot and maybe one other spotlight that moved from Keith as he was doing a backup voice to Brian as he was doing the solo. Bill was often not in the light at all. Charlie could hardly be seen." Mankowitz steered away from using a flash because the band didn't like it, and he himself felt it deadened the atmosphere. However, this created problems: "The lighting was often so bad I couldn't actually take pictures. That's one of the reasons why I used to stand at the back and shoot out into the spotlight — to try to capture the atmosphere."

Different areas of the country reacted differently to the Stones: "The fans didn't really discriminate: They screamed at me as well, and I was on the stage with the band most of the time. It was very, very, very exciting, but it was also a real eye-opener. In the Midwest and the South we felt as though we were really struggling and out of depth. In places like Memphis and Nashville and Raleigh and Shreveport, all the black acts on the tour — because the Stones insisted on Patti LaBelle and the Bluebells and the New Vibrations being support — had to stay in segregated hotels. Although they had experienced that before in '64, it was a real struggle."

Mankowitz observes of the tour as a whole, "It was full of periods of boredom and repetitiveness and exhaustion. Money didn't really begin to trickle down to the band until '66. There weren't great groupie scenes, there weren't parties every night, there weren't a lot of drugs. It was relatively modest and low-key."

In April 1966, the group would release the album *Aftermath* in the UK, the first LP to be exclusively cowritten by Jagger and Richards. That this transpired to be a semiclassic is astounding in light of Mankowitz's memories of its genesis. "They were under pressure to write because they were booked into the studio at the end of the tour," he says. "I had one long evening somewhere in the middle of the tour with Mick, just hanging out with him. I remember him saying words to the effect of, 'We've got twelve songs to write and it's really hard because of the schedule.' They would fly out straight after the show and get into the next place at two, three in the morning."

While Jagger and Richards had an album to compose, and Jones and Wyman enthusiastically sought out female company, Watts was at loose ends. Mankowitz says, "Charlie was a bit of a loner, anyway. He hated being away from [his wife] Shirley, and communicating then on the road was very difficult. He was continuously practicing with a practice pad. He was, quite curiously, insecure as a musician, and I think he was very resigned to the rigors of being on the road. A very nice man."

Mankowitz took a photograph backstage in Sacramento involving Richards that could conceivably have recorded the end of the band. Mankowitz: "None of the electrics were [grounded] — it was all two-pin.

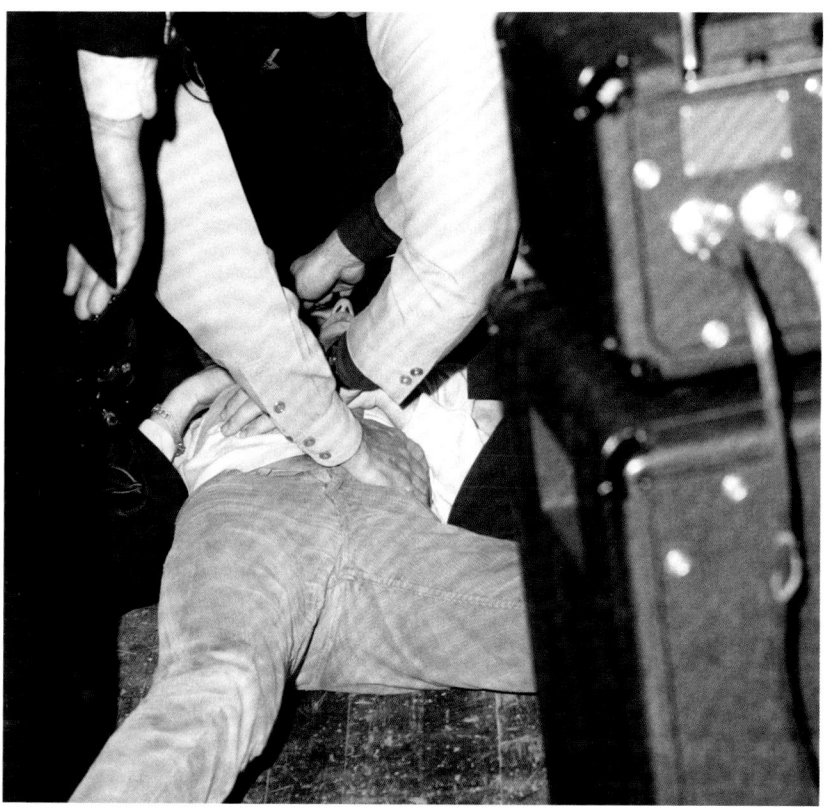

The microphone had swung off-center, and instead of moving it with his hand, he used his guitar. The metal strings touched the mic, which must have been live. There was this blue flash and this puff of smoke, and he just was thrown back among the backline amps. It was terrifying because for a brief moment we thought he was dead. Klein was there, and he nudged me and said, 'Get a shot.' [Keith] must have been out of it for a few minutes in order for me to have gone back to the dressing room, put my flash gun on, and take a picture."

In Hollywood at the end of the tour, Mankowitz shot some of the *Aftermath* sessions. "I had to be very tactful because a lot of the stuff I shot on a Hasselblad, which makes a terrible noise," he says. "I'd always keep out of the way when they were actually doing a take. Most of the stuff I did was during playback and run-throughs. I think I must have done the first two days of the recording before going home for Christmas."

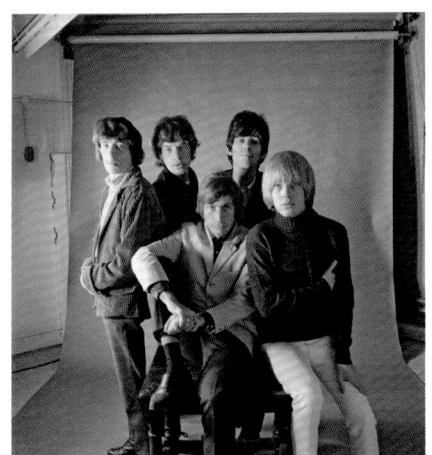

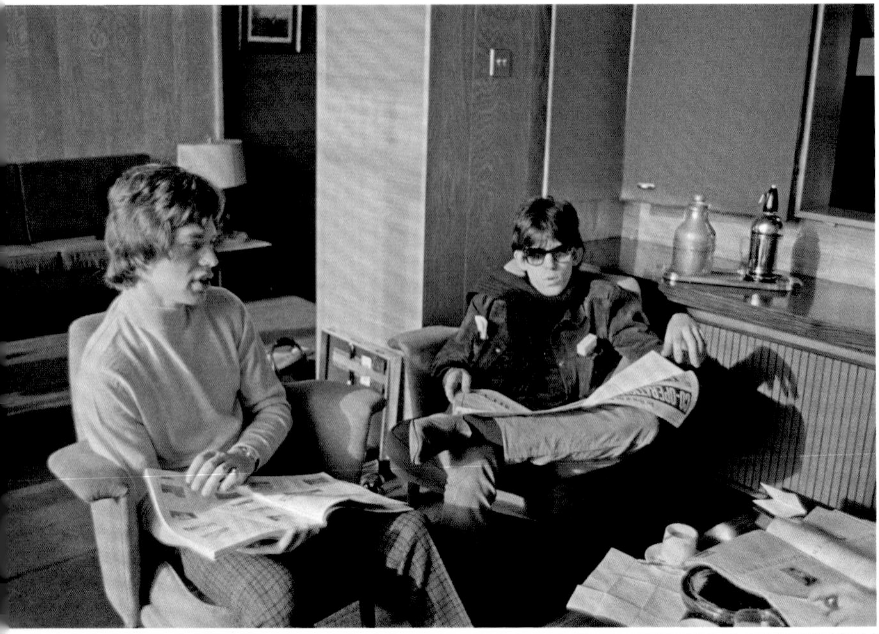

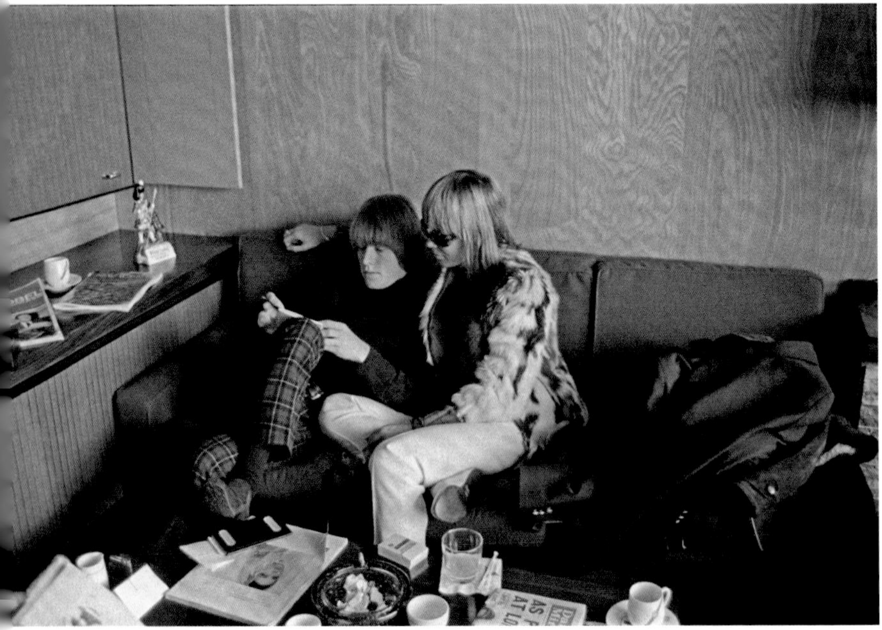

A crowded day for the Beatles

Redundancy
Payments

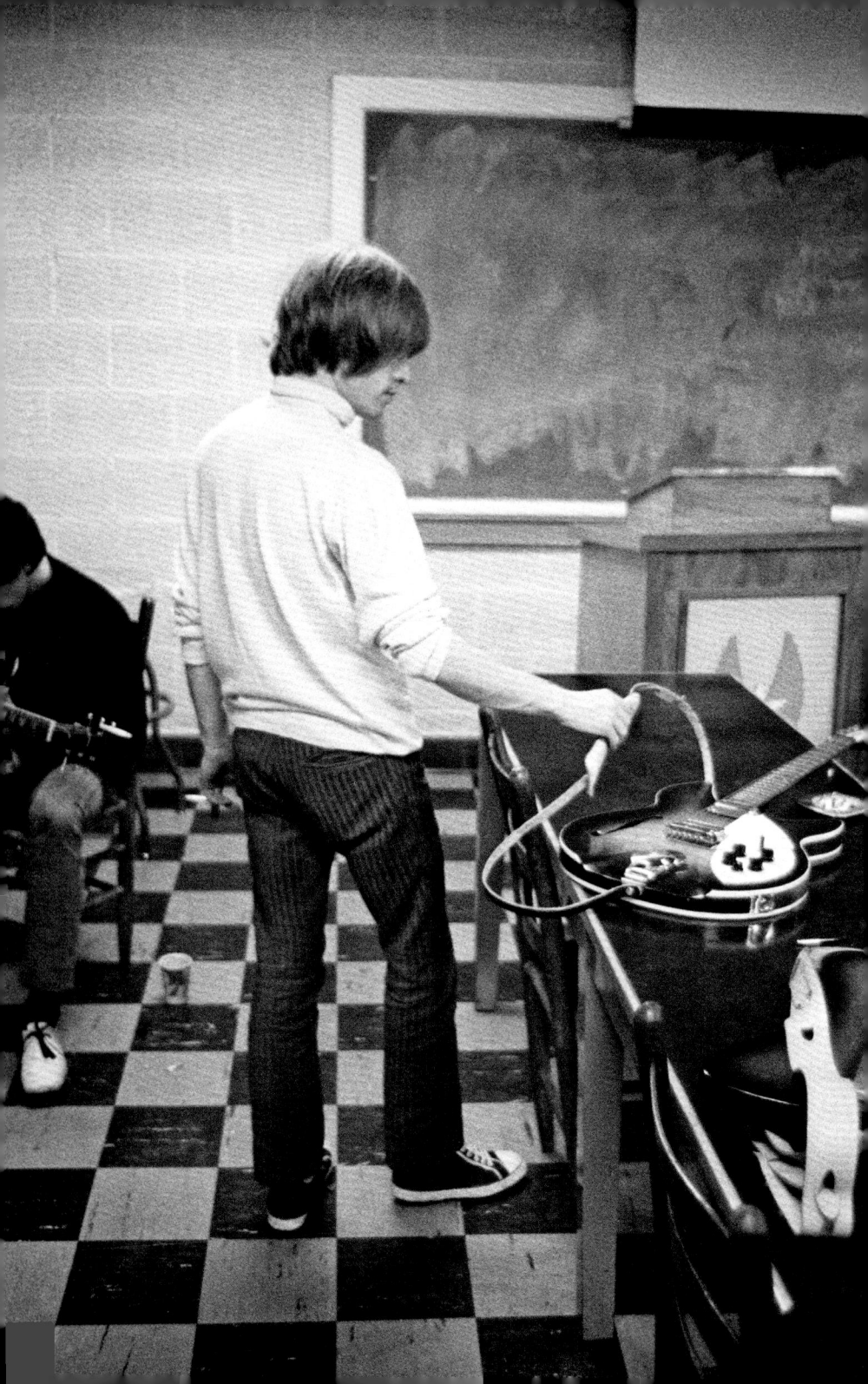

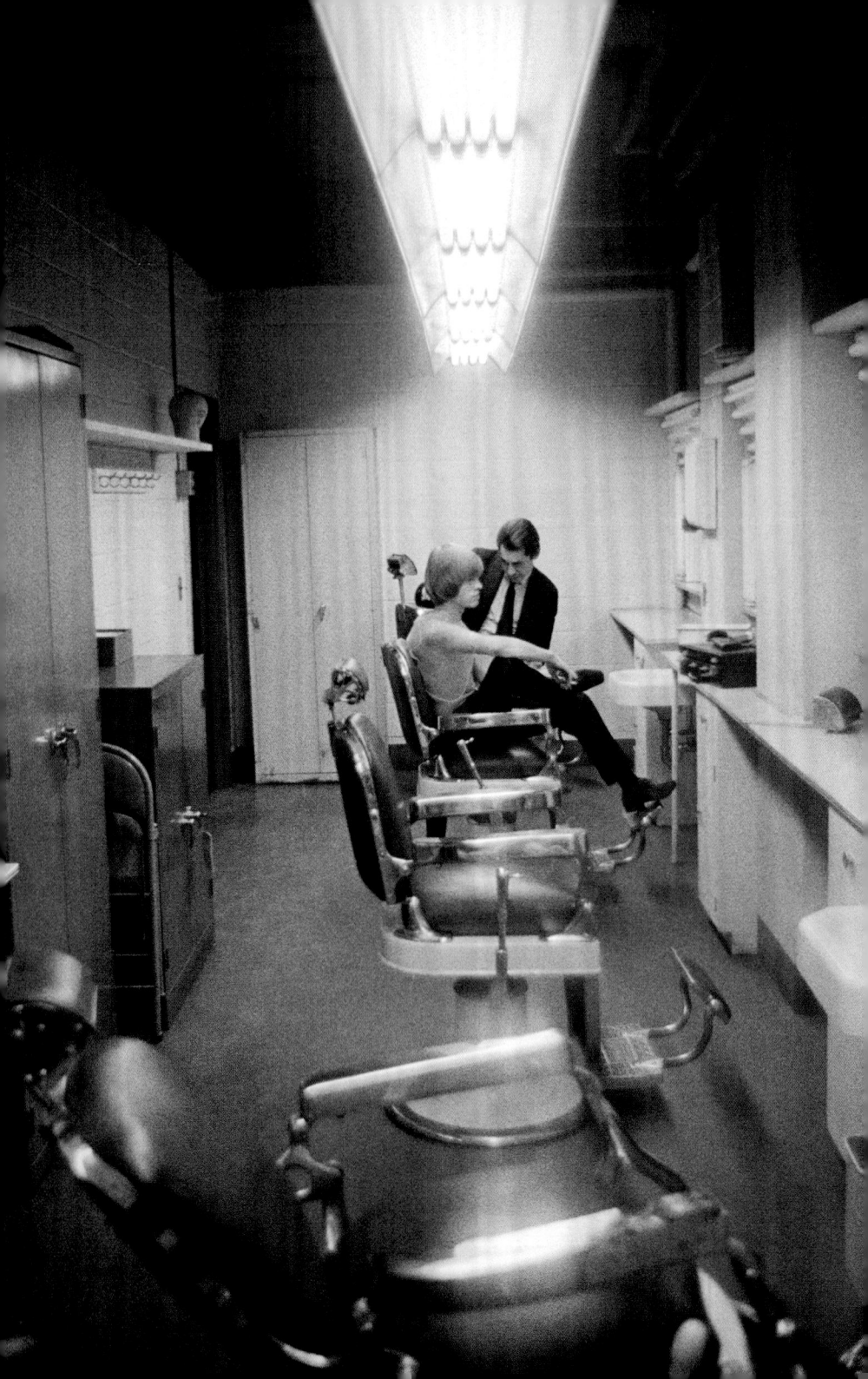

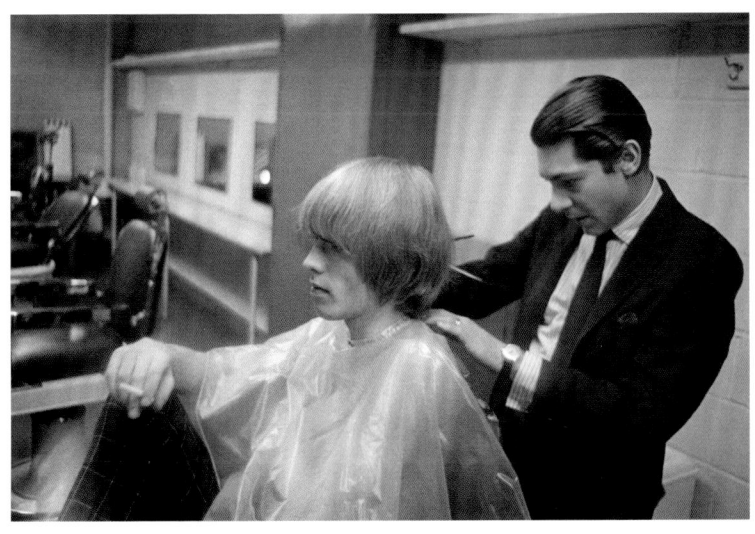

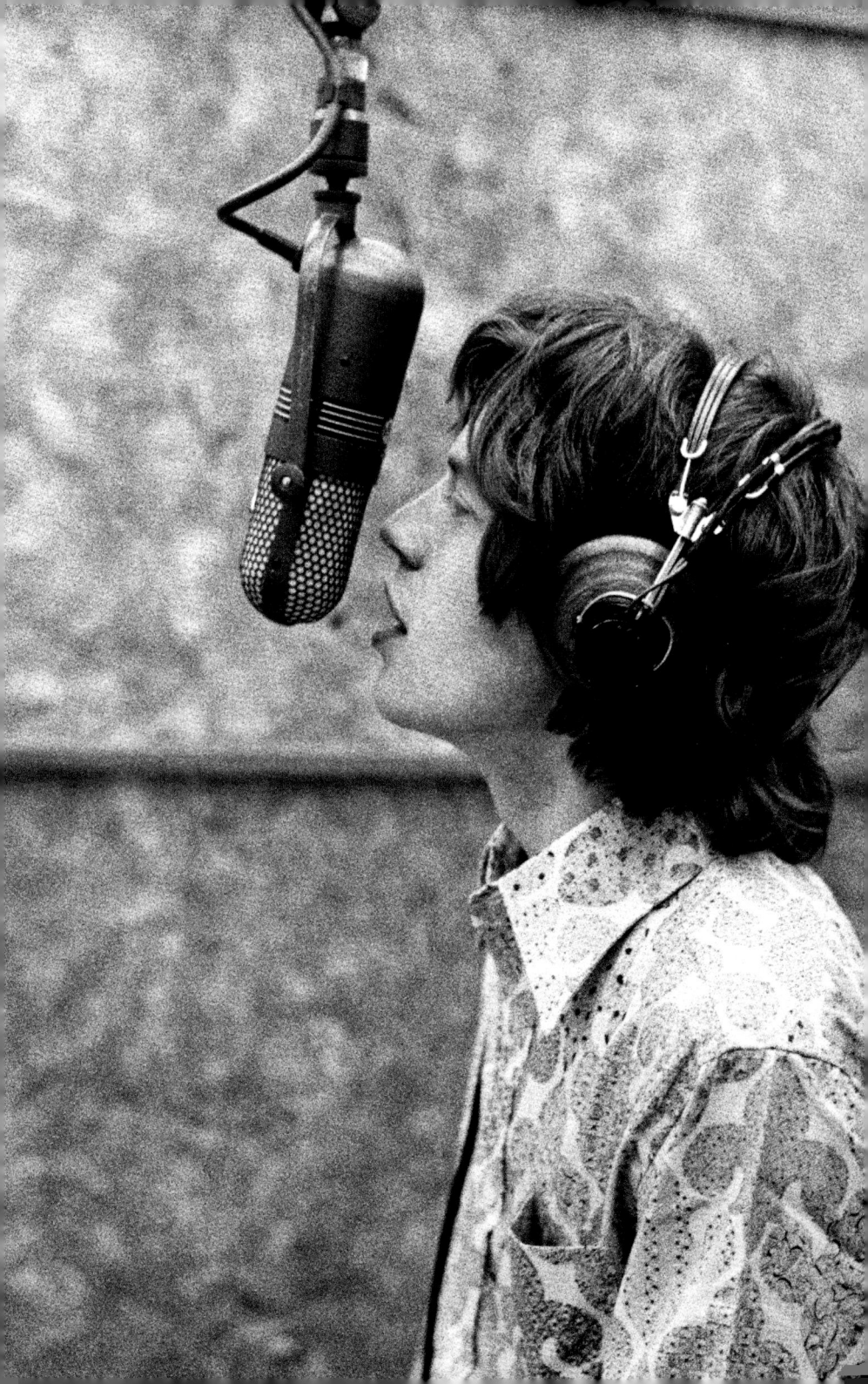

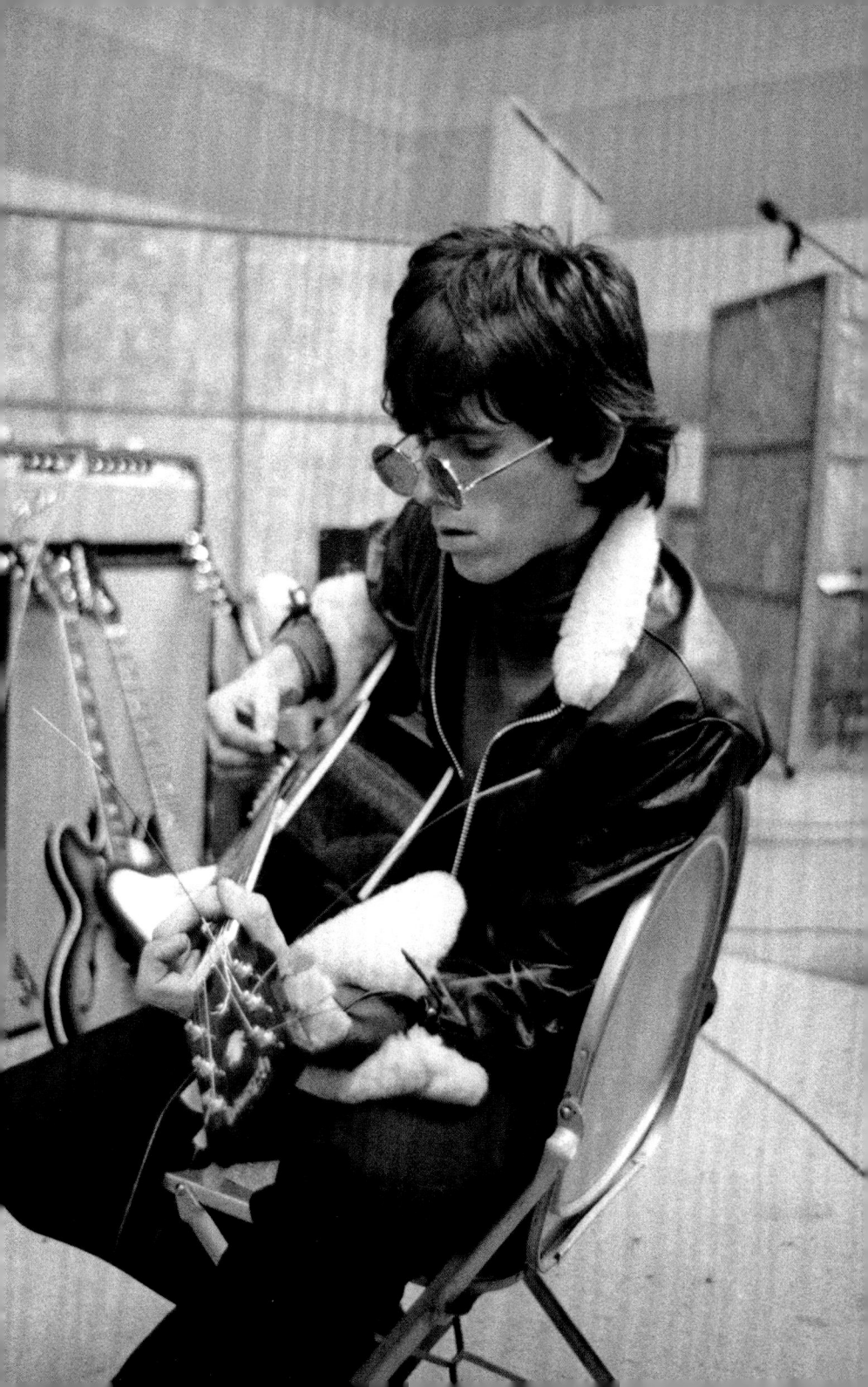

KLH 604D

1966

THE INCREASING SUCCESS OF THE STONES led to a public
demand for access that in some respects they were reluctant
to meet. As a consequence, in 1966 Mankowitz began snapping the group members in their private abodes. "Magazines
were beginning to want more intimate portraits of them," he
explains. "It was a pragmatic thing in as much as they really
didn't want strangers coming into their homes if it could be
avoided. So it was decided that I would shoot a session with
each of them." Richards's newly-bought Redlands house was
being gutted: "I did a shot of him sitting on a lavatory bowl
that was out on the lawn waiting to go in the house. There's
an edginess, a lack of respect for the format, that was a
Stones-ian take on it."

A gig Mankowitz photographed at the Albert Hall in September 1966 produced the sleeve of the in-concert album *Got Live If You Want It!*, which was released in the U.S. in December 1966. The front of the LP boasted a montage of the teen idols playing their music against a wall of screams. Mankowitz: "That was the big problem in those days: Because of the lack of organized, composed lighting and the impossibility of photographing a live performance from the balcony or something, it was almost impossible to get the whole band in a single frame. So I just said to Andrew [Oldham] I was going to make sure that I got solo pictures of everybody, and the collage montage was the obvious solution, but I didn't design it."

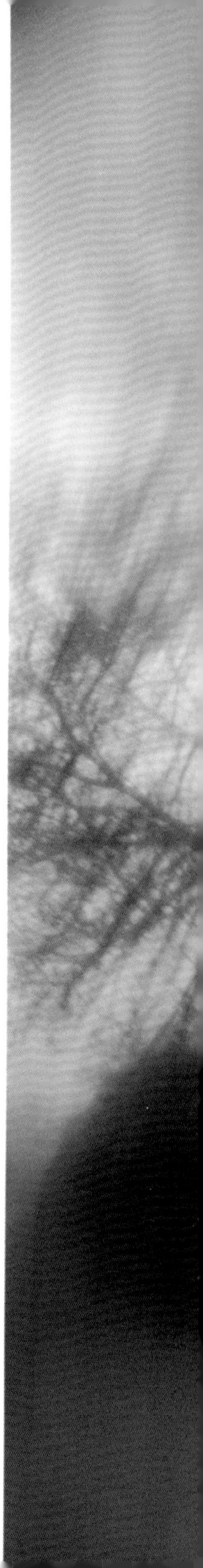

3

1967

THE BAND'S STUDIO ALBUM *Between the Buttons* was released in the UK in January 1967. A collection of curiously frilly tracks, it was something of a disappointment after the edgy *Aftermath*. Its jacket was in some respects far more interesting than the contents. Once again, Mankowitz secured the prestigious cover photograph after being usurped in that role by Guy Webster for *Aftermath*. Explains Mankowitz, "That's probably the peak of my period with the Stones because I felt the most confident. I was in a position where I could try and contribute something to the image of the Stones, using my photography to convey something about the mood of the time and the drug-infused culture that was beginning to emerge. So I made this filter with Vaseline and glass and black card, and I proposed that we do the shoot at the end of an all-night recording

"There was a strange decadent quality to them, but for photography they looked terrific."

session because I thought the band looked so Stones-ian at that moment — when you emerge stoned, bit hungover, bit exhausted, into the light of dawn. I took them to Primrose Hill, knowing that we were going to get something but not knowing for certain that it was going to translate into a cover. Andrew was behind me encouraging, teasing, keeping the atmosphere, because everybody was pretty exhausted. The whole session only lasted about twenty minutes." The combination of Mankowitz's considered technique and serendipity — Watts's blue tie and shirt set off perfectly a celeste sky — created one of the most beautiful images of the Stones.

Sixty-seven was the year the Stones became dandified, an initial image of floppy hats, candy stripes, and trailing scarves melding into the flower power fashions of the Summer of Love. It was all a far cry from the sullen collective style that was considered their forte in some circles. "I thought the Stones pulled it off," says Mankowitz. "There was a strange decadent quality to them, but for photography they looked terrific."

Mankowitz was present prior to the filming of the TV show *Sunday Night at the London Palladium* on January 22, 1967. During the program, the Stones caused outrage by refusing to mount the revolving podium at show's end to join in the traditional cheesy mass wave sign-off. Mankowitz: "I think Mick and Keith cooked that up during the day. Andrew thought it was a disastrous thing because, however rebellious they might have been, they needed to maintain the success. There was a certain degree of tension in the dressing room, but I don't remember any talk of it. It certainly made every single paper and was considered to be an incredible snub."

Combined with the heart-stopping sexual frankness of their latest single "Let's Spend the Night Together," this transformed the Stones in the eyes of powerful people from irritants to public enemies and led to a traumatic year. In February, the famous Redlands bust culminated in June with harshly discriminatory prison sentences for Jagger and Richards (subsequently quashed) and a campaign of harassment, possibly

involving planted drugs, against Jones. "It was a very upsetting period," says Mankowitz. "Klein came over to stage manage the responses. I got a message that said if the press called you, you say absolutely nothing that might compound the problems. It was quite scary. The establishment felt seriously threatened by the band, and that they'd gone too far, that they were a damaging influence on the youth of today. They were going to bring [the Stones] down."

The same year, Mankowitz lost his position as in-favor photographer to Michael Cooper, the result of a power play that occurred during the early sessions for the album *Their Satanic Majesties Request*. "The atmosphere was really, really strained," Mankowitz explains. "The guys would not arrive on time. Andrew was dreadfully unsettled by it. There were a lot more drugs about and a lot of strange people about. One night, Mick stormed into the control room and, in front of me, said to Andrew words to the effect of, 'Michael Cooper's gonna do the cover and this is what it is.' I knew that was me out. I never had problems with Mick — I photographed Mick later that year for a magazine — but I was firmly in Andrew's camp. I was working with Andrew on lots of other things, and the Stones were leaving Andrew." Mankowitz admits, "I don't think I was very unhappy. I'd started working with Hendrix earlier in '67, so it wasn't as though the Stones was my only gig. I had a pretty buoyant career."

As did the Stones. When Mankowitz next photographed the group, they were more gods than idols.

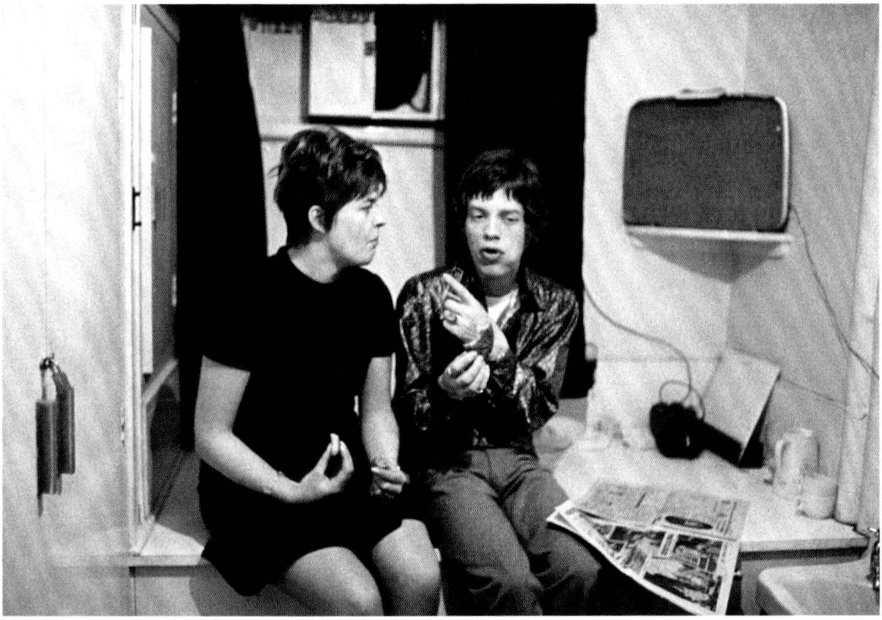

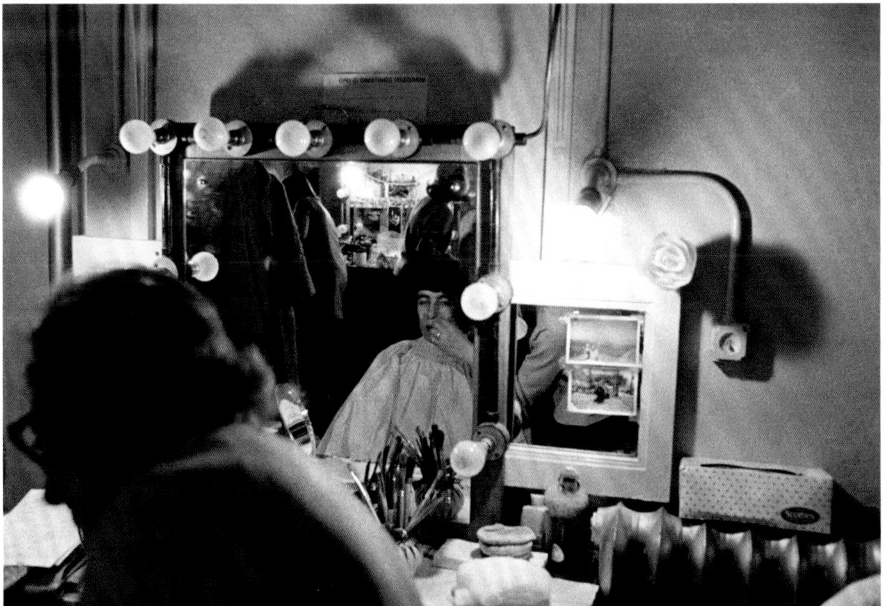

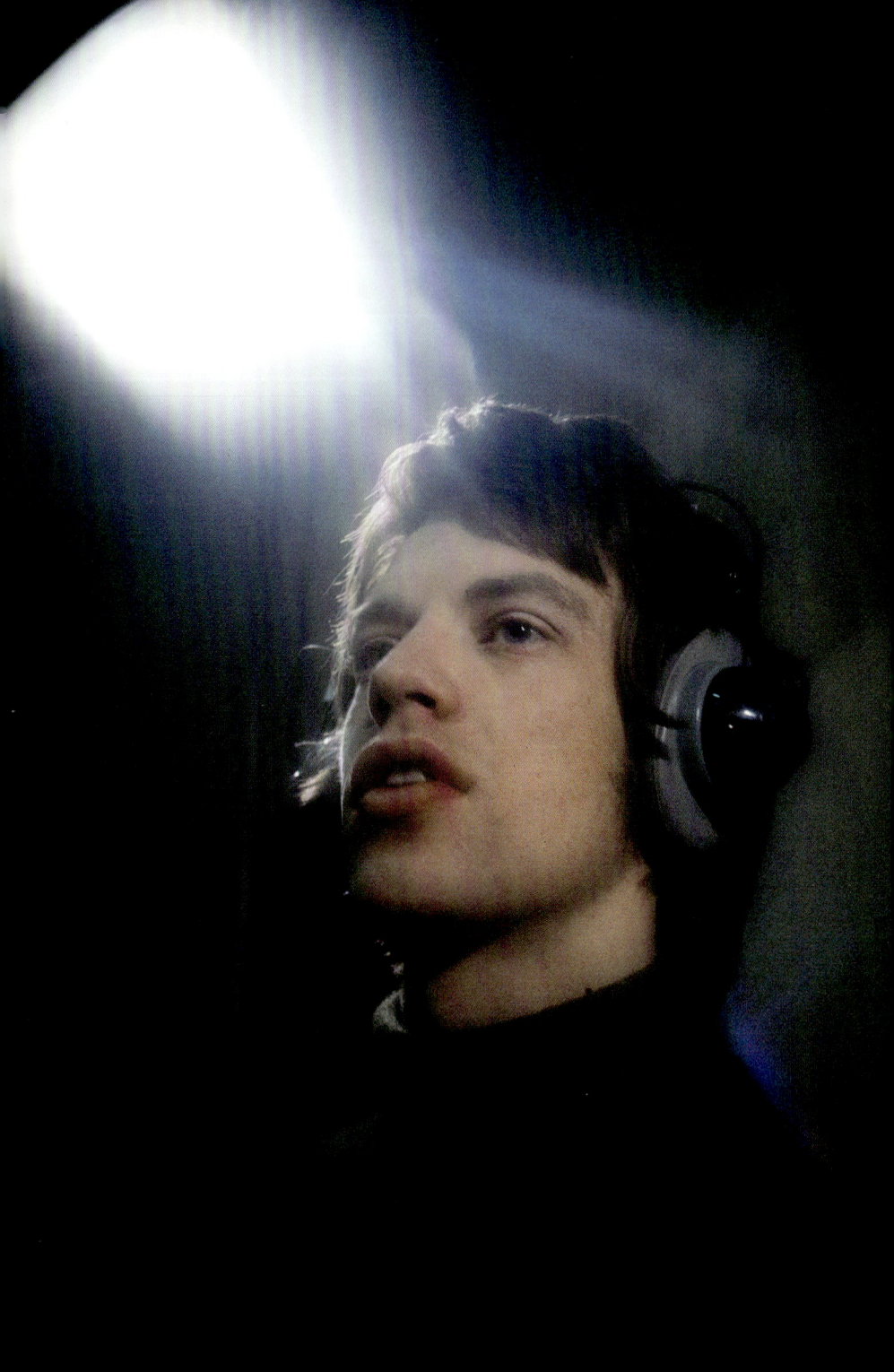

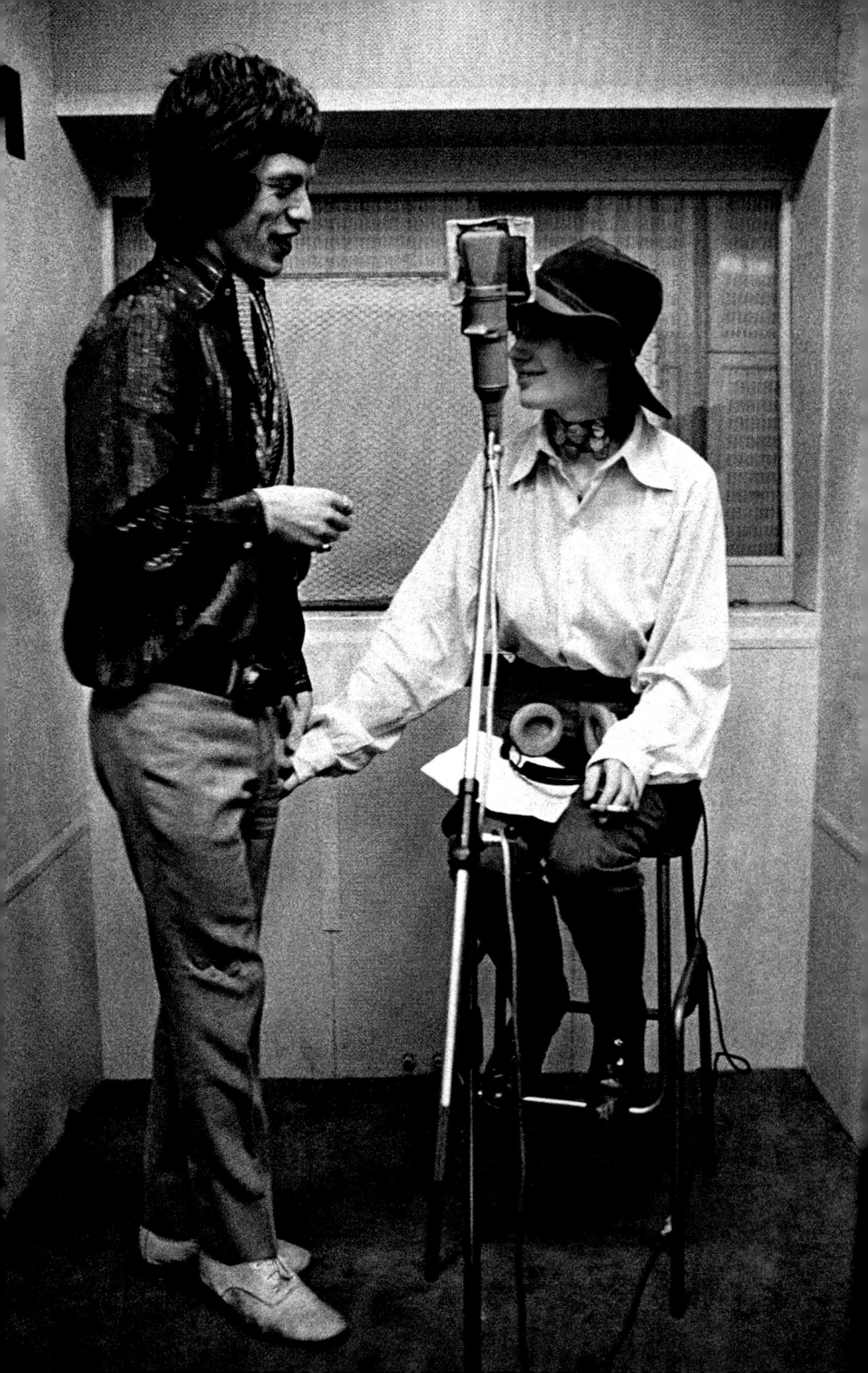

1982

BY 1982, THE ROLLING STONES had weathered time, tide, and drug busts and emerged as unassailable elder statesmen-cum-divinities.

So threatening to the authorities in 1967 that they had been victims of an attempt to crush them, the Stones were now themselves — at least in rock terms — the Establishment. Their rebellious mien had been diluted over the course of the seventies. They had been supplanted by a new generation, many of the social injustices against which they had once railed had been addressed, and their musical output now spurned the adventurism that was once their stock-in-trade. However, the public adored them more than ever. Their 1981 album *Tattoo You* had been hailed as proof-positive of their enduring viability, and the band was set to embark on a massive world tour to promote it.

Photo editor Colin Jacobson knew of Mankowitz's association with the Rolling Stones and asked him if he'd like to shoot the pictures for a planned feature in the *Observer*'s color magazine. Mankowitz found the idea of a professional reunion exciting, and the Stones were "very approving and supportive." However, he was pitched into unfamiliar and slightly bewildering territory. Ronnie Wood had by now replaced Mick Taylor, who had earlier replaced Brian Jones, but that was just the beginning of the changes in the Rolling Stones: "The environment and where they were in the hierarchy and the huge team of people that they had around them was mind-blowing. They were at Shepperton Film Studios, but it was all veiled in secrecy. We were told that we would be given an address to drive to, and then we would be guided by another vehicle to where they were rehearsing. It was so bullshitty it was ridiculous."

Mankowitz found the band welcoming, but the conditions were less-than-optimum. Jagger requested that Mankowitz not use flash, just like the old days. "Inside this huge soundstage, the band was set up with a huge sound system but no lighting, just awful cold sulphurous lights in the ceiling," Mankowitz recalls. Additionally: "There must have been fifty people hanging around." As well as the large payroll of crew and backing musicians, the room contained assorted family members: "It was a strange, unreal atmosphere. I just cut myself off from everything that was going on around and tried to focus on the band. We worked through the night, and it was absolutely wonderful to be with them again and to be photographing them. I got some rather good pictures of them in spite of the light and everything."

Mankowitz never got the formal group shot he needed for the magazine cover. He says, "What was extraordinary, in two nights my entire, original two-and-a-half years with them was replayed: this great warm feeling on the first night — we drove home through the dawn feeling high and happy — and then the next time it was like the '67 break-up again. The office did call me and I went back two nights later. I'd found

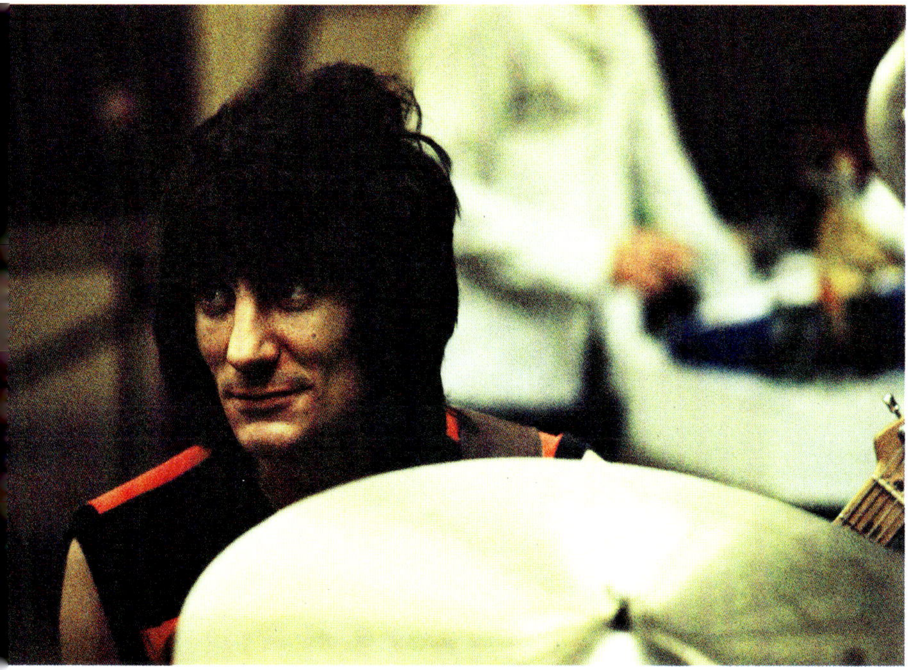

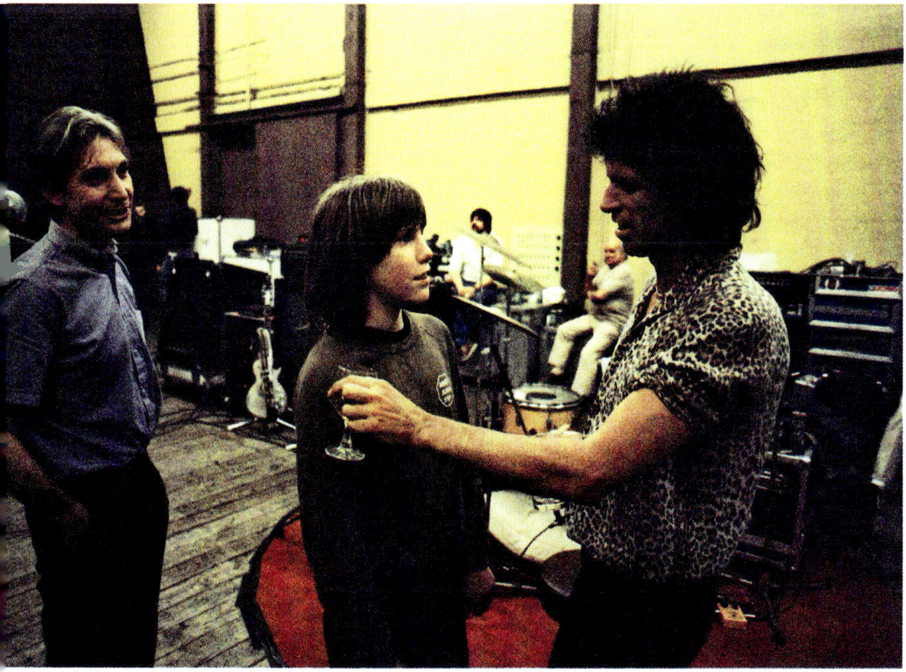

1982

a green room with a huge battered sofa and a very distressed wall, and I decided that I was going to line them all up. Finally at about two o'clock in the morning, Mick turned up very drunk and very angry and shouted at me, 'What the fuck are you doing here? It ain't gonna fucking happen!' Then Keith turned and said to me, 'All you do is remind us of the very bad times, man.' It was awful. I never, ever, ever was able to establish what had gone wrong."

Mankowitz suspects it might have been the price he had cited when sounded out by a Stones courtier about becoming the tour's official photographer. He says, "I got enough pictures the first night to satisfy the *Observer*. I was dreadfully sad I didn't get the formal portrait 'cause it would have been a great coup for me. It was clear in 1982 that the world they now occupied had nothing to do with the world that I'd known them [in]. They were not the same people I knew."

The last time Mankowitz met the Stones en masse was at the February 1986 wake of their roadie and original member Ian "Stu" Stewart ("They were very friendly but I didn't photograph the evening"). He says, "I have a good relationship with the Stones office because it's important for me to be able to have a dialogue if I have a project to discuss. Other than that, "I haven't seen them and I don't really want to. What it used to be was so terrific, I don't really want to spoil that memory."

As to his overall feelings about having photographed the self-proclaimed Greatest Rock 'n' Roll Band in the World, Mankowitz says, "I'm thrilled, overjoyed, that I had that wonderful opportunity. It was an extraordinary period in my life, and I do think I did some good work." That good work, and the legacy of Mankowitz's short but close involvement with the band, continues to be unexpectedly viable, for the Stones have carved out a uniquely elongated fifty-year career. Jokes Mankowitz, "When people said to me a few years ago, 'Oh my God, how do you feel about the Stones still on the road?' I used to say, 'I think it's very generous of them to continue to promote my photographs.'"

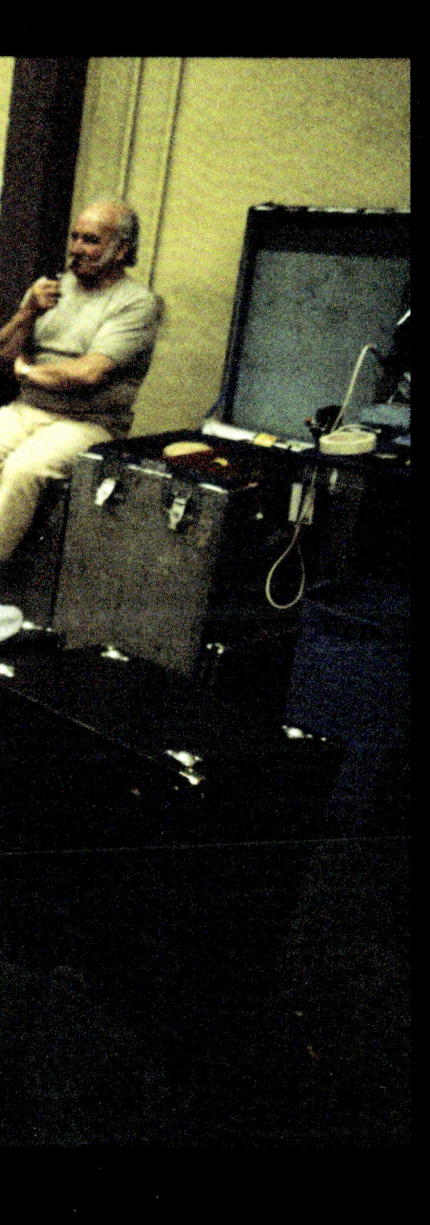

ACKNOWLEDGMENTS

I WOULD LIKE TO THANK Andrew Loog Oldham and the Rolling Stones for their trust, confidence, and friendship.

My wife, Julia, and my daughters, Jessica and Rachel, for their endless support.

And all at Insight Editions for the great job they have done in producing this book.

—GERED MANKOWITZ